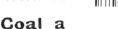

BYGONE
GODSTONE

High Street in the early 1900s.

BYGONE
GODSTONE

Juliette Jaques

Phillimore

1992

Published by
PHILLIMORE & CO. LTD.,
Shopwyke Hall, Chichester, Sussex

ISBN 0 85033 816 6

Printed and bound in Great Britain by
BIDDLES LTD.,
Guildford, Surrey

UVEDALE LAMBERT
1870—1928

To the memory of Uvedale Lambert,
father of Godstone Local History;

and to Jean Tooke for her encouragement
and unfailing enthusiasm

List of Illustrations

Frontispiece: High Street, early 1900s

Acknowledgements

Illustrations have come from a variety of sources. The majority are family photographs or Edwardian postcards lent by local collectors. Others are from libraries and institutions. I am indebted to the following for permission to reproduce pictures: Miss J. Bates, 84; J. J. Browne (Jewellers) Ltd., 98-100; Mr. N. Catford, 148-9; Mrs. M. Corbin, 128; Mr. M. Cowie, 3, 115, 137, 157; Mr. A. A. Crowhurst, 132; Mr. A. G. M. Davis, 89; Mr. R. Fairall, 153-5; Mrs. J. Faulkner, frontispiece, 7, 21, 37, 76, 80-1, 138; Mr. J. Gent, front cover, 1, 112, 135; Mr. and Mrs. T. F. Goad, 82; Miss L. Ketteringham, 60; Miss A. Knight, 4; Mrs. Miles, 96-7, 111; Mr. D. Moore, 57; Mr. and Mrs. F. J. Ohlson, 14; Mr. R. Packham, 2, 5, 6, 8-12, 15, 17, 19, 20, 23-32, 35-6, 38, 42, 45, 49-51, 61-4, 74, 77-9, 83, 93, 95, 101-2, 113-14, 116, 124, 127, 130, 141, 156, 160-3; Mr. G. A. Smith and Mr. M. Smith, 13, 16, 18, 22, 33-4, 39-41, 46-7, 52-4, 75, 105-6, 108, 118-19, 121-3, 125, 129, 131, 134, 136, 139-40, 144-5, 158-9, 164-6; Mrs. B. Millican, Mr. and Mrs. P. Stacey, 126; The Domestic Buildings Research Group (Surrey) for their drawings, 14, 19; Felbridge School for their permission to use pictures which appeared in Gordon Wilkinson, *The Village School* (1983), 167-70, 172; The British Geological Survey, 146-7, 150; Surrey Local Studies Library, 43-4, 48, 58, 107, 109-10, 120, 151-2; Surrey Record Office, 117.

I am grateful for cooperation and help from the following: Miss E. Bryant in showing me her study about the influence of roads on Godstone; Godstone parish church of St Nicholas and the Rev. C. J. Studdert-Kennedy for allowing me to consult the parish magazines and for lending me the portraits of the Hoare rectors; Mr. G. Brooks for reproducing the Vestry portraits of the Hoare rectors; Mrs. N. Hanlon for information on the Godstone Institute, now the Club; the Club for lending me two pictures; Mr. and Mrs. Askew for information about sport; Mr. C. Foxon for information about bowls; Mrs. Goad for permission to use illustrations from her grandfather's book, Uvedale Lambert's *Godstone: A Parish History* (1929), and her father's booklet, Uvedale Lambert's *Godstone: A Short History* (1982); Mrs. E. Bushby for the maps; Mr. P. Sowan and Mr. P. Burgess for helping me to find and annotate pictures of the mines and quarries.

Finally, I am grateful to many people, too numerous to mention by name, who have talked to me about the traditions of Godstone and 'the old days'.

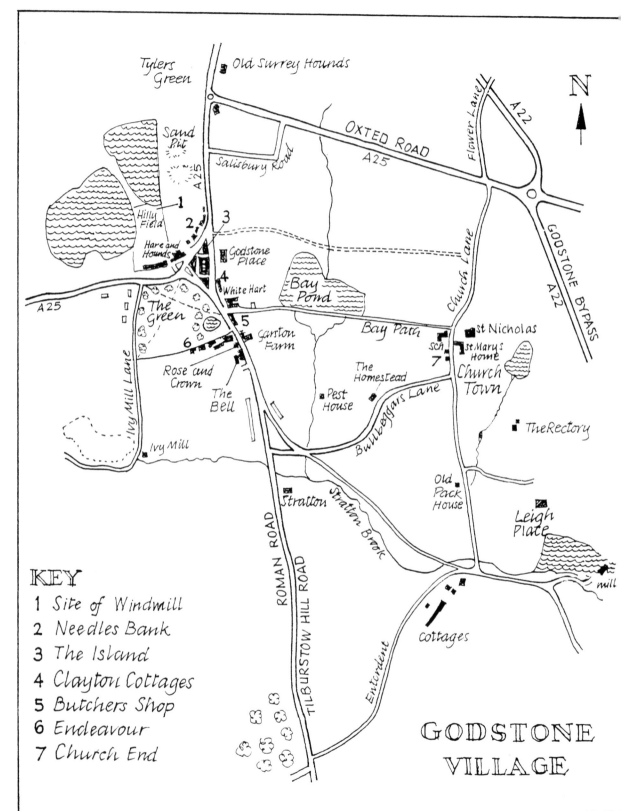

Tylers Green

Old Surrey Hounds

OXTED ROAD

A25

Flower Lane

A22

N

Sand Pit

Salisbury Road

1

Hilly Field

2

3

Hare and Hounds

Godstone Place

4

White Hart

Bay Pond

Church Lane

GODSTONE BYPASS

A22

A25

The Green

5

Garston Farm

Bay Path

St Nicholas

Sch

St Marys Home

7

Church Town

6

Ivy Mill Lane

Rose and Crown

The Bell

The Homestead

Bullbeggars Lane

Pest House

The Rectory

Ivy Mill

Old Pack House

Stratton

Stratton Brook

Leigh Place

mill

ROMAN ROAD

TILBURSTOW HILL ROAD

Enterdent

cottages

KEY

1 Site of Windmill
2 Needles Bank
3 The Island
4 Clayton Cottages
5 Butchers Shop
6 Endeavour
7 Church End

GODSTONE
VILLAGE

E. Bushby

Introduction

The village of Godstone lies in the south-east of Surrey. Its position is comparable with that of more than a score of towns and villages along an east-west line just south of the North Downs. This corresponds with a spring line, and thus a plentiful water supply.

Boundaries of the parish of Godstone have varied over the years but its shape, a long narrow strip about two miles wide, a characteristic which it shares with the neighbouring parishes of Tandridge and Bletchingley, has not altered. The original object of this great length was probably that every parish should have its share of good and bad soil for cultivation and wastes for hunting.

Godstone originally extended 13 miles from its northern boundary to Felbridge on the Sussex border in the south. The present parish only stretches down to the south side of Blindley Heath.

The heart of Godstone, its most ancient part, consists of two centres, now the two conservation areas, of contrasting character (see map of Godstone Village). Church Town is quiet and secluded, with old timber-framed buildings. The earliest is the Old Packhouse which dates probably from the 15th century. The only stone used generally in the houses was for the sandstone foundation walls, white hearthstone appeared in the late 16th century and can be seen in the chimney of one of the old cottages of Church Lane. In the 18th century brick became the fashionable material for house building, two fine examples of which are Church End and Church House, opposite the church.

With the growth of wheeled traffic in the 16th century, Godstone Green became a busy centre of roads and vehicles which demanded the establishment of Godstone's numerous inns. Exposed timber-framed building is rare in the village although many of the older buildings are timber-framed structures. Many have had brick or hearth stone fronts added. A number of new houses built entirely of brick appeared in the 18th century, notably the row in the High Street, best viewed from across the pond on the Green. In the very core of the village is a triangular island, at one time enormously populous and containing an endless variety of houses with yellow sandstone and white hearthstone walls.

The two parts of Godstone are linked by Bullbeggars Lane, a narrow road leading from the south of the village to the church, and the footpath running from the *White Hart* and its barn, along Bay Pond to Church Lane.

To the north of Godstone, on the west side of the main road, were the windmill on Hilly Fields and the now disused sandpits. On the east side also were sandpits until the building of Salisbury Road at the turn of the century. Further along are Tyler's Green and the 20th-century council estates to the east and west. We now come to the Godstone junction 6 of the M25 and pass under it to Godstone Hill, on the other side of which are the now disused stone quarries. To the west and north is Marden Park, for so long the seat of the Godstone lords of the manor (see map of Godstone Part 1).

Going southwards from the village (see maps of Godstone Parts 2 and 3) we can take the Roman road running straight as a die up and over Tilburstow Hill to Blindley Heath,

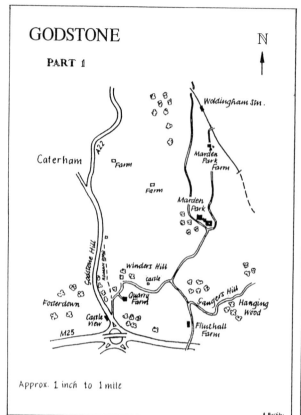

GODSTONE

PART 1

Caterham

Approx. 1 inch to 1 mile

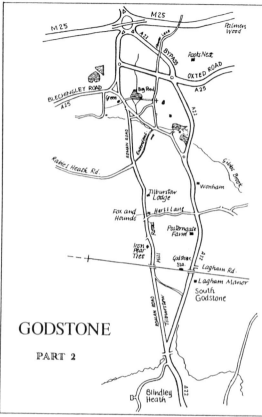

GODSTONE

PART 2

or the lower road constructed in 1839 to avoid the steep gradient of the hill. This takes us to Godstone station, built in 1841, on the line from Redhill to Tonbridge, and round which sprang up the houses of South Godstone. Just past the railway line to the west stands the ancient manor of Lagham. Further south, and now no longer part of the parish, is Felbridge, at the juncture of Surrey and East Sussex, where once stood the home of the 18th-century Evelyns, including James, who endowed the school which still remains active to this day, and is one of the oldest primary schools in the country.

Godstone was not the original name of the parish. Both village and church are called *Wolcnestede* in the earliest Saxon documents. The nearest a Norman clerk could get to it was the spelling *Wachelstede* which appears in Domesday Book, 1086. Later we find *Wolkenstede*, *Walkhamstead* and *Walkinstead*. The name fairly certainly denotes the fulling place where men used to trample wool in a trough filled with fuller's earth to remove the grease. Eustace of Boulogne's Flemish followers who came over in the 11th century may have recognised the word 'walken' meaning to full. It was in later centuries that *Godistone*, *Godestone*, or *Coddestone* slowly took the place of the ancient name. The most likely explanation is that it represents Goda's tun or farm which Goda brought as a marriage portion to her second husband, Eustace of Boulogne. Goda was the daughter of Ethelred II, who died in 1016 and who held land at Walkingstead.

The Roman road ran north-south, coming from London via Croydon over Godstone Hill, through what is now the village and straight up Tilburstow Hill and on to the south.

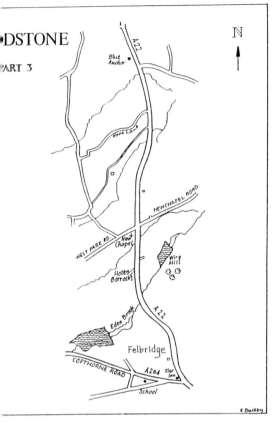

Parts of the old Roman surface have been found some feet below the present road. However, this paved road was deserted after the Romans left England and in Saxon days the favoured route was through Church Town and so up the hill by a lane now called The Enterdent, which was no more than a sandy track until the Second World War.

Church Town was the old *Wolcnestede* where the Normans built a stone church, probably replacing a timbered edifice. In later days, however, the old Roman road came into its own once more when houses were gradually built around Godstone Green. By Elizabethan times the village on the green was already of more importance than the hamlet by the church. To this day the two parts of Godstone, Church Town and the Village, remain quite distinct.

The country round Godstone was settled by the Saxons at least as early as the sixth century. The earliest mention of Godstone occurs in two 10th-century Saxon wills. In Domesday Book the entry for Walkingstead reads as follows:

The lands of Count Eustace in Tenridge Hundred ... The Count himself holds Wachelstede, Osward held it of King Edward. It was then assessed for 40 hides, now for 6. There is land for 30 plough teams. In demesne there are 3 plough teams, 39 villeins, 2 borders with 22 plough teams. There are 10 serfs, and one mill worth 6 shillings and 3 acres of meadow and wood worth 100 hogs. To this manor belong 15 dwellings in Southwark and in London worth six shillings and 2000 herrings. In King Edward's time it was worth 20 pounds, afterwards 16 pounds, now 20 pounds. Yet it renders 28 pounds by weight.

Uvedale Lambert, in *Godstone: A Parish History* (1929), analysing the Domesday entry, estimates that the settlement would have comprised about fifty-five families or a population of some 275. The houses in Southwark and London represented a liability to defend the City of London and the herrings were payment made by the occupants of the houses to Count Eustace, from the herring fleet catch landed in the City.

Eustace supported William the Conqueror in 1066 and was rewarded by the gift of many manors in England. His grandchild, Matilda, married Stephen, King of England 1135-54. From the troubled period of Stephen and Matilda few records relating to Godstone can be found. Its history comes to life again two or three generations later during the reign of Henry II, with the lordship of Reginald de Lucy. Reginald was in all probability the brother of Richard de Lucy, famous as Henry II's justiciar.

Reginald's son, Richard, who succeeded to the lordship of Godstone, gave the southern half of the manor to his sister, Margaret, and her husband, Odo de Dammartin, who established their manor at Lagham. The northern half was given to his older sister, Lucy and her husband, Roger de St John, who founded the manor of Marden. The two manors came together again when Alice, daughter of Odo and Margaret, sold her manor to Roger de St John, son of Lucy and Roger. In the disastrous Black Death of 1349 which swept off probably about one third of the population of England, de St John, lord of the manor, died. The inquest on his lands shows how Godstone was devastated, for it lists among other items:

> A water mill rickety and ruinous, worth nothing this year because all the customers who used to grind at it are dead so that there is no custom and it stands empty and no one will rent it. Perquisites of court are worth nothing this year because the tenants who used to do suit are dead.

Roger de St John who succeeded to this pitiful inheritance hastened to dispose of it in 1351 to Sir Nicholas and Margaret de Loveyne. Margaret was the widow of a rich London citizen, Sir John Pulteney, four times Lord Mayor of London.

From the Loveynes, Godstone passed to the St Clairs and the Harcourts. In 1566 Simon Harcourt conveyed it to Thomas Powle of London, clerk to the Court of Chancery who, in 1588, sold it to George Evelyn of Long Ditton and Wotton.

A new era opened for Godstone during the Evelyn lordship when it became one of the chief places in England for the manufacture of gunpowder. Until 1562 gunpowder had had to be imported as one of its constituents, saltpetre, was not obtainable in this country. Then Queen Elizabeth I entered into a contract with a German captain who had sought refuge in England from religious persecution in his own land. For the sum of £300 he agreed to teach the English the secret of the manufacture of saltpetre.

George Evelyn became one of the few owners of mills where gunpowder could be made under licence. He and two of his sons, John and Robert, were engaged in the business. With the acquisition of Godstone, while continuing production at Long Ditton, they either took over an enterprise begun earlier by the Lees of Leigh Place or started their own manufacture at Leigh Mill which continued until 1636.

A number of Evelyns, all descendants of George Evelyn, are connected with Godstone. The Evelyn family is a large one and the proliferation of Johns can be confusing. George Evelyn was born in 1526 at Kingston upon Thames. About the year 1550 he married Rose Williams. From this marriage John, the second son, born about 1556 and Robert, the third son, were both engaged in powdermaking.

George's second wife was a Mrs. Rogers, a young widow whose maiden name was Joan Stint. They had a son, Richard, who became the father of John Evelyn, the diarist.

John, the powdermaker of Godstone, married Elizabeth Stevens. Their second son, John, of Lee Place, M.P. for Bletchingley in 1627, 1628 and 1640, was knighted by Charles I in 1641 and buried in Godstone in 1664. He had married Thomasine, daughter of William Heynes of Chessington. Their second son, also John, born 1633, inherited Lee Place, Stratton, Marden, Rook's Nest and Flore House. He was created a baronet in 1660. This Sir John was wild and extravagant. He mortgaged his property to build a new house at Flore where he eventually lived with his mistress, Mary Gittings, leaving his wife at Leigh Place. In his will Sir John conveyed all he could to his mistress.

The part of the manor which Sir John Evelyn could not leave to Mary Gittings passed to his brother, George of Nutfield. George's second son, also named George, succeeded him. Like his father, George sat in Parliament for Bletchingley from 1708-24. He was buried in Godstone aged 46 in 1724. He left three daughters only and so this branch of the Godstone Evelyns died out.

The heir on his death was his brother Edward. He bought much land around Felbridge and took over a house called Heath Hatch. This house no longer exists but his son, James, built a new mansion on or near the site. James is notable as the founder of a school for the children of the poor. It still stands today and is used as a primary school. Felbridge was part of the parish of Godstone until 1953.

To return to Mary Gittings. As soon as Sir John died she lost no time in realising her property, which she sold to Sir Robert Clayton and John Morris for £4,180; then she married Edmund Hoskings of Barrow Green. So began the Clayton lordship which was to last for 240 years.

Robert Clayton was born in 1629 at Bulwick, a small village in Northamptonshire. His father was a small tradesman and farmer. Robert was one of several children but the only one to become successful. He was apprenticed to his uncle, Robert Abbott, a scrivener. Abbott had amassed much wealth which he left to his nephew at his death. Evelyn in his diary for 18 November 1679, just after Clayton had been installed as Lord Mayor of London, writes:

> I din'd at my Lord Maior's, being desired by the countess of Sunderland to carry her thither on a solemn day, that she might see the pomp and ceremonies of the Prince of Citizens, there never having been any, who for ye stateliness of his palace, prodigious feasting and magnificence, exceeded him ... He married a free-hearted woman, who became his hospitable disposition.

John Evelyn always speaks well of him. On 12 October 1677 he writes:

> With Sr. Robert Clayton to Marden, an estate he had bought lately of my kinsman Sr. John Evelyn of Godstone in Surrey, which from a despicable farme house Sr. Robert had created into a seate with extraordinary expence. 'Tis in such solitude among hills, as being not above 16 miles from London, seems almost incredible, the ways up to it are so winding and intricate. The gardens are large, and well wall'd and the husbandry part made very convenient and perfectly understood. The barnes, the stacks of corne, the stalls for cattle, pigeon-house, etc., of most laudable example. Innumerable are the plantations of trees, expecially walnuts. The orangerie and gardens are very curious. In the house are large and noble rooms. He and his lady (who is very curious in distillerey) entertained me three or foure days very freely ... This place is exceeding sharp in winter, by reason of the serpenting of the hills; and it wants running water; but the solitude much pleas'd me. All the ground is so full of wild thyme, marjoram and other sweete plants, that it cannot be overstocked with bees; I think he had neere 40 hives of that industrious insect.

Robert Clayton died on 16 July 1707 at Marden. Having no children, he made his nephew William, son of his brother William, his heir. In 1732 William was created a baronet. Among his descendants, the 5th baronet, William Robert, born in 1786, fought under Wellington at Vittoria and at Waterloo, and became a general.

Marden was burnt down in 1879, and only the stables were left standing. Sir William Clayton, the 6th baronet, wanted to rebuild on a higher site but the tenant, Sir Walpole Greenwell, insisted on the old site. Sir William sold Marden and other Clayton lands in Surrey to Sir Walpole Greenwell, 1st baronet in 1911. His son, Sir Bernard Greenwell, died in 1939 and his son, Sir Peter, who moved to Suffolk, sold the whole estate in 1951, making the parish council lord of the manor.

In the old Wolcnested the Normans built a stone church, as mentioned above. The present church, however, gives scant evidence of such antiquity. It has been much altered during the years especially at the restoration in 1872-3 by Sir George Gilbert Scott.

The earliest known institution of a rector is in 1304, and the episcopal register goes no further back than that date. This first recorded admission is of Walter de Westerham.

Little is known of the early rectors beyond their names and approximate dates but by the 18th century there is more information. This period was notable for the laxity of the

Anglican Church and Godstone had its absentee, indeed infamous, cleric, in John Kidgell. According to the *Dictionary of National Biography*:

> he was a man of some talent, but dissolute and dishonest. James Douglas, Earl of March and Ruglen (afterwards the well known Duke of Queensberry) appropriately appointed him his chaplain. In May 1762 he was instituted to the rectory of Godstone. However he habitually neglected his duty and lived as a man about town.

Horace Walpole in his *Memoirs of the Reign of George III* terms him 'a dainty priggish parson, much in vogue among the old ladies for his gossiping and quaint sermons'. Kidgell became so deeply embroiled in discreditable political intrigues that he was forced to fly the country. No more was heard of him until 1794 when in Bonn, Germany, he signed a resignation.

Owing to his absence and neglect the parsonage had fallen into utter disrepair and had to be rebuilt. This was one of the first tasks of Kidgell's successor, Charles Edward de Coetlogon, a very different man. He was a popular and eloquent preacher, not untouched by the influence of John Wesley. He saw to the repair and upkeep of the church fabric and was caring of the needs of his parishioners. De Coetlogon died in 1820 and was buried in Godstone churchyard.

The gift of the incumbency of Godstone lay with Henry Hoare of Mitcham, the banker of Fleet Street, a man well known for the active part he took in supporting the great Church societies and other useful and charitable institutions of the day. Henry Hoare presented to the living his third son Charles James. Through his family connections, the new rector was in touch with the foremost evangelicals of the day, the most famous of whom belonged to the 'Clapham Sect'. This was a group of laymen, distinguished in various walks of life, who devoted much of their time and wealth to religious and philanthropic work. Charles James Hoare could count such people among his friends. Like many of them, he was conscious of the superiority in birth, wealth and education he possessed and the duty it imposed upon him to exert himself on behalf of the less fortunate members of society. He was interested in the work of the National Society for the Education of the Poor in the Principles of the Established Church and preached sermons in its support. In his own local sphere, it is evident from Godstone Vestry Minutes that during his long incumbency Hoare attended closely and conscientiously to the needs of his parishioners. He died at Godstone rectory in 1865, having been, one might say, the founder of a Hoare dynasty of rectors. He was to be succeeded by no less than four more bearing the name.

The population of Godstone had grown from an estimated 275 at Domesday to 1,081 inhabitants at the first census of 1801, slowly increasing in ensuing decades. *Pigot's Directory* of 1830 puts the figure at 1,397. It describes Godstone as 'a cheerful and pleasant little village, though not one of much trade, its chief prosperity being derived from its thoroughfare situation and agricultural business, besides having in its vicinity some excellent stone quarries'. This comment rightly characterises the charm of Godstone and indicates the sources of its prosperity, but does slight justice to its size. It was the most populous parish of the 14 parishes making up the Godstone Registration District and was an important administrative centre. The Petty Sessions were held in Godstone, while the Board of Guardians met at the *White Hart* to administer the Bletchingley Workhouse. Godstone's primacy was only challenged much later by the smaller surrounding parishes when they began to be developed due to the advent of the railway.

By 1901 the population of Godstone had risen to 2,800. Since then it has increased further with the building of several council estates and some private development. At the 1981 census the figure was 5,368. While some of Godstone's inhabitants undoubtedly commute to London or work elsewhere, Godstone has never become a dormitory town comparable in scale to Oxted, Caterham or Warlingham. It is one of the few villages within 20 miles of London to retain much of its rural character.

With the advent of coach travel, the favoured route from London to the south coast was the one roughly following the old Roman road through the Caterham gap in the North Downs, to Godstone and on to the south, hence the springing up of houses in Godstone on a north-south linear pattern. Inns flourished, the *White Hart* being the favourite posting house. At the beginning of the 19th century the road had improved and in 1808 a regular coach service between London and Brighton via Godstone was in operation. By the 1830s there were three daily coaches to London. In the opposite direction there was a daily coach to Brighton, a daily coach to Lewes, and one to Eastbourne three times a week. To avoid the long pull up Tilburstow Hill a new cut was made a little to the east in 1839, rejoining the Roman road at Anglefield Corner.

The railway never reached Godstone, the closest station being two miles to the south, on the cross country line between Redhill and Tonbridge. A station opened there in 1841, around which grew the hamlet of South Godstone. There were no direct links with London or Croydon until the Caterham line opened in 1856 and the Oxted line in 1884.

The coaches of the first half of the century were superseded by horse omnibus with a service between Croydon, Purley, Caterham and Oxted. Later another service ran between Godstone and Caterham. Not till 1912 did the motor bus begin to replace the horse bus.

Few people realise how important the stone quarrying and mining industry in Surrey once was. Its existence is certainly hinted at in our standard county histories but more precise details of its nature must be sought in the papers of learned societies. Paul W. Sowan, in *The Firestone Mines at Godstone*, published by the Croydon Natural History and Scientific Society (1976), deals specifically with Godstone.

In ten or eleven places under Godstone Hill, or to the east or west of it, hard or soft varieties of the greenish-grey calcareous sandstone of the Upper Greensand have been extracted for three distinct purposes: building stone – which may be seen in Quarry Farm and several cottages near the mines around Godstone Hill, in the walls and buildings in Godstone village, and in Walkingstead around the church, to the east of the main village; refractory stone (firestone) – used for the beds of glass furnaces, linings of lime kilns, ovens, hearth-stones (not to be confused with hearthstone); hearthstone – small rough, or cut, or moulded, blocks of soft friable Upper Greensand which, when wetted, were used to rub on stone floors, steps or hearths, leaving a chalky white deposit. The use of rough lumps of stone was later superseded by sprinkler cartons of hearthstone powder sold under such trade names as 'Snow-Drift Step Powder' and 'Osowhite Step-Powder'.

Aubrey, in *The Natural History and Antiquities of the County of Surrey* (1718-19), contains perhaps our earliest specific mention of there being stone quarries at Godstone.

The Evelyn family held Marden from 1588 to 1671 and, as has been seen, had interests in the manufacture of gunpowder at Godstone; whether they also concerned themselves with stone mining is not known. Although Aubrey's mention of it indicates that quarries had for some time existed at Godstone, it appears that these really developed on a rather larger scale when the Marden estate passed to the Clayton family in 1672.

Oral tradition in the 1880s and 1890s appears to indicate that a date around 1720 was of some significance in the quarries' development.

It was about 1820 that mining of hearthstone for whitening was started. The term 'mining' is used advisedly, as extraction techniques are quite distinct from those of quarrying. The difference is still recognisable underground, where one can walk from quarry to mine and see the exact demarcation line between the two. During the 1870s to 1900s working faces were exploited simultaneously for both products – hearthstone from top of the face, building stone from middle/bottom – so these galleries were quarries cum mines.

The reports of the Mining Records Office for 1858 give two entries for the Godstone mines: 'Sir William Clayton (freeholder) Mr. Stenning (Quarryman). Firestone used for buildings and repairing roads. Firestone for glass furnaces, hearthstone etc. Nearest Railway Station or Shipping Port: Godstone'.

The advent of the railway favoured the stone industry in the Godstone area, easing the problems of transport. It is about one and a half miles to Caterham station from Godstone Hill and three and a half miles to Godstone station. Business prospered and the scale of Victorian hearthstone quarrying was extensive. By the 1890s Godstone was producing some 4,000 tons of saleable stone per annum and employing up to 18 men.

Then in the early 20th century came a decline. Employment figures fell and some disused galleries in the quarries were devoted to mushroom growing. During the Second World War, parts of the quarries were used for secure storage by the London Hospital, the Natural History Museum, and by various wine and spirits merchants.

Ownership of the mines passed to the Greenwells when Sir William Clayton sold his estate to them in 1911. Work continued to diminish in the '20s and '30s. In 1942 Horace Fairall, of Rose Bank, Godstone, took over the mines which remained open and some hearthstone was still being sold as late as 1950. Work seems to have terminated soon thereafter.

Sand has also been another source of local income. It has been used for building, for cleaning purposes (sanding floors of pubs and shops), and instead of blotting paper in early days. The Claytons owned sandpits in the village, at The Enterdent and on Tilburstow Hill. The Fairalls exploited a sandpit at Taylor's Hill. Their sand was used for building and for the protection of London houses from fire bombs in the Second World War. Gravel was dug too. Henry Rose had a pit on the Tilburstow Road in the 19th century.

In the very recent past (1983), Conoco, a major oil company, obtained permission to sink bore holes at Palmer's Wood, between Strete Court school and the M25. These proved successful and the next year further boring took place on the same site. So oil may be Godstone's future industry.

Bibliography

Andrew, Arthur, *Godstone in 1900* (1980, Godstone Preservation Society)
Bourne Society, *Local History Records. Vols. I-XXX*
Evelyn, Helen, *History of the Evelyn Family* (1915)
Fairall, Horace, and the Scouts, *Glorious Godstone* (1934)
Gray, Peter (ed.), *Godstone Explored* (1975, Tandridge District Council)
Lambert, Uvedale, *Godstone: A Parish History* (1929)
Lambert, Uvedale (son of the above), *Godstone: A Short History* (1982)
Victoria County History

The Green

1. Godstone Green in 1898. The pond was then a horse-pond with a sloping bank down which the wagoners drove their horses. In the centre of the picture, the pedestal surmounted by a ball is a memorial to the Claytons. It was eventually removed as it was so often uprooted and thrown into the pond by Victorian vandals.

2. The *Clayton Arms* or *White Hart* occupied an early 16th-century building opposite the pond. Originally the *White Hart* in the 18th century, it was called the *Clayton Arms* after the Lords of the Manor.

3. Two brothers, Alfred and John Butcher, appropriately named, stand in front of their shop opposite the pond and next door to the *White Hart* yard. They are listed in a 1905 directory.

4. In 1901 R. G. Knight had opened his butcher's shop in Caterham. By 1910 he also had this one in Godstone which was run by his brother.

5. A row of 18th-century brick cottages at the southern end of the village in the 1940s. It adjoins what is now the Godstone Hotel and Coachhouse Restaurant. The cottage to the right, rendered and with a sign over the door, is Curd's Tea Rooms which used to be a favourite meeting place for cyclists in the 1920s and '30s.

6. Garston Farm is shown on the right of this photograph taken in the 1940s. It was a 16th-century building re-fronted with bricks and tiles about 1700. Originally the *Greyhound Inn*, then Greyhound Farm, its southern aspect has been altered to reveal the timber framing. The firestone wall has been removed. It is now the Godstone Hotel and Coachhouse Restaurant.

7. The Garston Farm cows going home from milking in the 1940s. Farmer Rice regularly drove them out onto the Eastbourne Road, across the Green, and over the A25 Bletchingley Road through the gap in Green View to the fields beyond to graze.

8.   A 1940s' view of 65-9 High Street, formerly Clayton Cottages. The extension to the first cottage on the right was a barber's salon, now demolished. An 1839 directory lists **William Brooker**, hairdresser. At the other end was Charles Brooker, newsagent's and tobacconist's, known for nearly a century as Brooker's. Charles Brooker III retired a few years ago and has since died.

9. Green View in the 1940s. Houses on the north side of the Green built by Sir Walpole Greenwell in 1913. At the end of the row is a track leading up to Hilly Fields and a Saxon barrow used in the 19th century as the base for a windmill.

10. This 1905 postcard shows a well-defined track running diagonally across the Green from the pond to the corner of Ivy Mill Lane. This was formerly a rope walk, where rope for plough lines, bells, scaffold cords, etc. were made. Between the A25 and this path stood posts round which the rope was wound. These were used for quoits games until the 1920s.

11. At the corner of the Bletchingley Road and Ivy Mill Lane which bounds the west side of the Green, stand North House and South House, a pair of houses built by Henry Rose in 1852. They are seen here *c.*1945.

12. A general view of the west side of the Green seen from the pond. This photograph was taken in the 1940s.

13. The south side of the Green in the 1950s. From left to right: North View, Yew Tree Cottage, Club Cottage and the Club House.

J. HARDING 16.82

14. North View. Drawn and recorded by Joan Harding and others for the Domestic Buildings Research Group (Surrey) in 1982.

EAST END

The Island

15. Aerial view of Godstone, taken in the 1930s, clearly showing the triangular island, which, in Victorian times, was densely packed with a quite remarkable number of cottages intersected by alleys. It is said once to have been the worst slum in Surrey, but now no longer, as much care and attention has been lavished on each dwelling.

16. Dove Cottages. Inside the island an alley runs behind the houses facing the Green, at the southern end of which is Puck's Cottage, which has medieval origins, and at the top end of which are Yew Tree Cottages. Between them used to be this row of tiny cottages, demolished in the early 1950s.

17. An early picture of the pond, *c*.1900, showing the High Street running north, and the west side of the Green. The shop in Acton House, the large house facing the Green, belonged to the grocer, George Burnell, whose name is preserved in Burnell's Cottage in the alley behind. The little building to the right is Ebenezer Goodwin's bakehouse.

18. Kelsey's bakery under construction at the beginning of the century. Goodwin's bakehouse was pulled down and a house and bakery were built by Richard Kelsey, the miller at Leigh Mill. Further along is the fire engine house, once used as the cage or village lockup. The crew were summoned by ringing the fire bell housed in a small belfry at the top of the gable. This century the building was for some years the office of the Parish Council.

19. The north-west tip of the island, known as Plum Cake Corner. The building just behind the telegraph pole is a small garage and filling station run at the turn of the century by Arthur Miles, carrier and fly proprietor. Eventually it became a café. The little brick cottages next to it were called Bull's Head Row. Behind them stood the village pound.

20. The first two-storey building on the left is Forge Cottage, notable for the use of the local white firestone in its construction. Further along is the village store and Post Office, sometimes called Hall's Stores after the family who ran it. Earlier Thomas Rose had been grocer and postmaster. When in 1840 the Penny Post was introduced it was he who received the first delivery. This photograph dates from the 1940s.

High Street and Needle's Bank

21. Godstone High Street looking north in the 1930s. To the right are the boundary wall and trees of Godstone Place.

22.   The great wall of Godstone Place, a striking feature, running all along the east side of the High Street. It is made of squared blocks of firestone, coped with brick. In this 1960s' photograph, the figure looking over the wall is Chad Stacey, a tree lopper and smallholder at Wonham Cottage, and a well-known character in the village.

23.   Behind the wall stands the present Godstone Place where once was a Tudor mansion owned by Nicholas Ashton. It was sold to the Evelyns in 1591.

24. The Bay Pond, *c*.1920. The present Godstone Place was owned by the Lindley family in the early part of this century. Its grounds included the Bay Pond, which Miss E. J. Lindley gave to the Surrey Naturalists Trust in 1965.

25. The Bay Pond walk, linking the village to Church Lane and the church. This picture dates from the 1930s.

26. A pre-1905 view of the High Street at the Bletchingley Road junction. Arthur Miles was a carrier. This shows his premises at the northern tip of the island in the High Street. Beyond is Needle's Point, later known as Needle's Bank, so-called after a John Needle who flourished there in 1704. John Gillings was the baker on Needle's Bank in Edwardian days.

27. The High Street and Needle's Bank in the 1940s. Arthur Miles has now been replaced by Teago Stripp, the butcher, and Gillings by A. Hall, baker.

28. Needle's Bank in the 1940s. Albert Hall, baker, has been succeeded by Edgar Hall, his nephew. Further along is Denny's Stores, a grocer's. Mr. Gould, a chemist, married Mr. Denny's daughter and for some time the shop was a chemist's on one side, and a grocer's on the other. Eventually it became entirely a chemist's.

29.   The end of Needle's Bank in the 1940s showing a sweet shop and tobacconist next to Denny's Stores. At the beginning
of the century it was run by an old lady in a wheelchair, Mrs. Abbots.

0. The northern end of the High Street in the 1940s. Lancaster's butcher shop, Fairall's and William Way's depots.

1. A charming row of 18th-century houses adjoining Needle's Bank on the A25 road to Bletchingley, seen here in the 940s. Next to the bakery from right to left: Tyle Cottage; Bankside, a perfect little Queen Anne House; and Rosebank, nce the home of Horace Fairall, a leading Godstonian, active in developing the sandpit at Taylor's Hill, and the business the village, now a builders' merchants. He was a very popular scoutmaster before and after the Second World War. e died in 1956.

32.   Further along the bank on the Bletchingley Road, 1907. In the middle distance on the east side of the High Street is Cavern House, so-called because it had an entrance, now blocked up, to the sandpits. It was once occupied by Rice Brothers, the harness makers. To the right is the northern apex of the village's triangular island.

33.   Headquarters of Christie's the builder, *c*.1900. Before his business was established the building was a malthouse.

34. A gang of Godstone builders at the turn of the century.

35. Salisbury Road in 1915. A new development started at the end of the 19th century.

36. The *Corner House*, *c*.1920. Soon after Salisbury Road comes the A25 turn-off to Oxted. It seemed almost certain that the Caterham railway would be extended to Godstone. So the *Godstone Railway Hotel* was built, later to become the *Corner House*, a residential hotel. In Edwardian times it was the home of Mr. McOwan who built on to it a small extension in which he ran a small private school. The building was pulled down in the 1950s and replaced by a block of flats.

Tyler's Green

37. Tyler's Green before 1905. Going north from the High Street in the London direction, we come to Tyler's Green, so-called because a family called Tiler from Bletchingley settled there in the 16th century. The area was then a waste in the manor of Bletchingley. A council estate was developed there in 1950-1.

38. Tyler's Green, London Road looking north, before 1906.

39. An Edwardian photograph of Tyler's Green, showing on the right the Baptist chapel, built in 1882 and rebuilt with a porch in 1973.

40. H. Stacey, baker and grocer. Mrs. Harriet Stacey's shop served the hamlet of Tyler's Green from about 1882 to 1905.

41. The Kateleys of Tyler's Green were renowned for their thatching of hay and corn stacks and their wattle hurdles were much in demand for sheep pens in the early years of this century. Their two sons who are decorators and do building repairs still live in the family home.

Inns

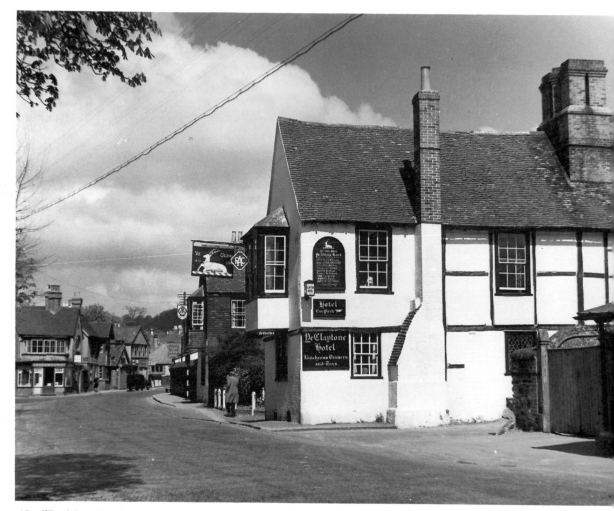

42.   The *White Hart* in the 1940s. In the 18th century it was called the *Clayton Arms*, and in later times its sign bore the Clayton Arms on one side and the White Hart on the other. It is a good early 16th-century building.

43. Inside the courtyard of the *White Hart* in the early 1900s. This space has now been incorporated into the ground floor.

44. Entrance to the *White Hart* in the early years of this century, here called the *Claytone Hotel*.

45.   The *Hare and Hounds*, shown here *c.*1904, on the north side of the Green: a favourite place for the hunt to meet. The building has altered very little through the years.

46. The *Bell*. In spite of 18th-century and Victorian additions, and a fire in 1909, this is probably the oldest Godstone inn. Some of the timbers at the rear date from the early 15th century.

47. The *Rose and Crown*, c.1905, now an insurance office. It is a timber-framed building of about 1500, covered by 19th-century tiles and bricks.

48.   The *Old Surrey Hounds* from a water-colour sketch by John Hassell. It probably dates from the time when Col. G. H. Nevill lived in Flore House and kept the hounds at Marden. Col. Nevill was Master of the Surrey Hounds from 1808-12.

49.   The *Fox and Hounds*, Tilburstow Hill, dates from the 17th century and is pictured here in the 1930s. In 1601, at Godstone Petty Sessions, Thomas Hart, Victualler, had his licence renewed. The Harts were an old Bletchingley family, well-to-do tenants of Pendell Manor. They also occupied Nash's Farm on Tilburstow Hill and gave their name to Hart's Lane, Godstone.

The Enterdent and Tilburstow Hill

50.   Looking down on The Enterdent from the hill above, *c*.1930. Part of the hill has literally been dug away, as it was the site of a sandpit exploited by the Claytons from the mid-1860s to 1871. The origin of the name Enterdent has never been satisfactorily explained. It is perhaps the dene or valley between two hills. There are a handful of houses at its eastern end.

51. Church Lane and the church seen from The Enterdent, *c*.1930. Tall trees now obscure this view.

42. The most substantial house on the Eastbourne road at The Enterdent. It looks Georgian but is probably earlier in origin. It was tea rooms and a hotel from the 1920s to the 1940s.

43. A gypsy encampment on Tilburstow Hill in the 1920s. It was popularly thought that one of the earliest cottages in The Enterdent was built by Polly Payne, a gypsy, and the little settlement was called Polly Payne's Bottom.

54. Hop picking under Tilburstow Hill.

55. Tilburstow Lodge in 1908. In 1855 it was the residence of Rear Admiral Fanshawe. Some time thereafter it burned down. By 1866 Henry Rose, miller, maltster and farmer of Nash's Farm nearby, was registered as owner and occupier. The lodge was rebuilt and by 1869 was in the ownership of Mr. Neil McVicar Forbes. Renamed Orme House, it was for some years this century a school and now has been modified to provide multiple dwellings.

56. Iron Pear Tree House, Tilburstow Hill, South Godstone, was so-called because in the garden there stood a pear tree which bore abundant but iron hard fruit. This picture shows the Georgian front.

57. Iron Pear Tree House showing Victorian additions at the side and back, and the family in the garden with their penny farthing bicycles.

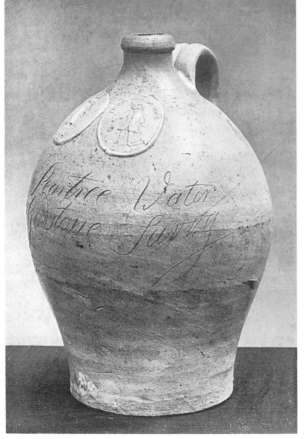

58. A magnificent Fulham stoneware jug made in the first half of the 18th century. It bears the inscription 'Drink and be well. Iron Peartree water, Nr. Godstone, Surrey'. This water, which came from a well in the garden, was thought to have curative powers. It was bottled, and sold in London at 6d. a quart. It could also be purchased at the *White Hart*, Godstone 'The Poor' could have the water *gratis*.

The Church and Church Town

59. St Nicholas' church from a John Hassell drawing of 1821.
Manning and Bray, the historians of Surrey, writing in 1809,
describe it as 'remarkably neat and well fitted up'.

60. The pulpit in St Nicholas' church, 1825, after Edward
Hassell.

61. An aerial view of St Nicholas' church as it is today. The north aisle was built about 1845. Sir George Gilbert Scott's complete restoration of the church in 1872-3 involved widening the chancel arch, inserting a new north side to the chancel, new windows to the nave and east end, and adding the south aisle. Later a new vestry was built in the angle of the south and east ends.

62. At the turn of the century, a finely carved screen was put up across the chancel in memory of Henry Gerard Hoare of Stansted. This was removed in 1974, allowing a nave altar to be used, in accordance with modern liturgical thinking.

63. The porch at the south door of St Nicholas' church, in the 1940s.

64. St Nicholas' church and churchyard, showing its pleasant setting in a view taken from the Rectory Pond, in the 1940s.

55. *(above)* Charles Edward de Coetlogon, rector of Godstone 1794-1820. Soon after his ordination he was appointed assistant chaplain to Martin Madan of the Lock Hospital near Hyde Park Corner. Madan was a lawyer turned divine, due to the impression made upon him by the preaching of Wesley. During his time with Madan, de Coetlogon became known as a popular and eloquent preacher.

56. *(above right)* Charles James Hoare, rector of Godstone 1820-65. Third son of Henry Hoare of Mitcham, he was presented to the living by his father in whose gift it lay. He founded what might be called a Hoare dynasty. No less than four of his descendants became rectors of Godstone.

57. *(right)* George Tooker Hoare, rector of Godstone 1865-81, and third son of Charles James Hoare. The chief event during his incumbency was the complete restoration and alteration of the church by Sir George Gilbert Scott.

68. *(above left)* James Samuel Hoare, rector of Godstone 1881-1903. Brother of George Tooker and fifth son of Charles James. Towards the end of their father's long incumbency either James Samuel or George Tooker would take the chair at Vestry Meetings; occasionally the brothers did it jointly

69. *(above)* George Edward Gerard Hoare, grandson of Charles James, rector of Godstone, 1903-30.

70. *(left)* Kenneth Gerard Hoare, son of George Edward Gerard, and rector of Godstone, 1955-65.

71.   Godstone Parsonage from a John Hassell drawing of 1821. John Kidgell, the 18th-century rector, through absence and neglect, allowed the building to fall into ruins. It had to be rebuilt in 1794 by his successor Charles Edward de Coetlogon. One suspects that de Coetlogon was something of a sacerdotal Horace Walpole and wanted a rectory in the gothick manner.

72.   Godstone Rectory, c.1910, and as it remained until 1953. The 19th-century Hoare rectors had large Victorian families to accommodate so they added an upper storey to the house as well as sundry outbuildings.

73. In 1944, Godstone Rectory and the glebe land were sold into private hands and The Homestead in Bullbeggars Lane purchased for use as a parsonage house which it remained until 1990. In the 1950s, the old Godstone Rectory, now called Glebe House, was restored to its two-storey origins, and crenellations were substituted for the rather bleak parapet.

74. A 1940s' view of the war memorial in the churchyard, and also the lychgate erected in memory of the first four Hoare rectors, 1820-1930. It was restored in 1978 to mark the 50th anniversary of the ordination of Kenneth Gerard Hoare (rector 1955-65). Beyond, on the other side of the road, is Church House, an attractive 18th-century dwelling, said to have been two houses, built back to back for two brothers, a builder and a curate, who did not have much in common – there was only one connecting door at the top of the stairs.

5. Godstone church bell-ringers in the late 1890s. Left to right, front: Brothers Green (jobbing builders), Herbert Galyer (carpenter), Chad Leigh (blacksmith), Fred Keatley; back: Brothers White (farm workers). The Godstone Parish Magazine for January 1894 records: 'On Thurs. 11th Jan. the Choirmen and Ringers came to supper at the rectory. Such a lot of pleasant fellows could not do otherwise than spend a thoroughly pleasant evening even apart from the roast beef and plum pudding'.

6. In 1872, Sir George Gilbert Scott, who was restoring the church, designed the almshouses for Mrs. Mabel Hunt of Vonham House, in memory of her only daughter who had died at the age of sixteen. They include eight self-contained houses, a warden's house and a beautiful little chapel, dedicated to St Mary. In this picture, taken in 1909, an Edwardian gentleman pays a visit to two ladies.

77. The north end of St Mary's almshouses in the 1940s. Built in a Victorian Tudor/Gothic style, the flèche-capped chapel and the gables compose a pleasing group with the church spire in the background.

78. Wonham House, home of Mrs. Mabel Hunt (who commissioned the almshouses), pictured here in the 1940s.

79. The steps from Church Lane up to the memorial for both world wars in St Nicholas', photographed in the late 1940s.

80. Church End and Potter's Cottage, in Church Lane opposite the almshouses. This view was captured in 1907.

81. The Old Pack House, Church Lane. An early 15th-century 'hall house' which had chimneys and floors introduced *c*.1600. Some 13th- and 14th-century pottery found in the garden indicates that it stands on the site of an earlier house, and it was at one time an inn. This picture was taken in 1905.

82.   An aerial view of Godstone school. In 1854 a piece of land opposite St Nicholas' church was made available by Sir William Robert Clayton and his lessee, Edward Stenning of Godstone, for a National School to be built for the sum of £1,451: There were four schoolrooms and a residence for the teacher consisting of a parlour, kitchen, scullery and three bedrooms.

83.   The back view of Godstone school in 1903, seen from the path running from Church Lane along the Bay Pond to the village.

84.   A class of pupils at Godstone school, *c.*1914, with their teacher, Mr. Thomas Bassett.
    Left to right, front row: Dollie Ball, ? Smith, Jessie Bates, Nellie Sadler, Jessie Moore; second row, Dollie Potter, Edie Coster, Nellie Bates, Amy Bryant, Edie Bates, Ada Gibson, Rosie Ball, Frances Hedges; third row: Edith Batchelor, George Gamlin, George Dumville, Bonnie Rice, Fred Brooker, ? Wicks, Fred Killick, Sophie Moore; back row: Percy Biss, ? Smith, Bert Killick, George Day, Horace Batchelor, Ernie Neal, Bill Gamlin, Bill Gibson, Jack Potter, ? Burberry, Chad Stacey, Mr. Bassett.

The first number of Godstone parish magazine. From its inception there was a printing press at Godstone school which was operated by pupils. In 1867, when the church launched a parish magazine, the first and last pages were printed on the school press. The magazine was devoted to matters of local interest, and the advertisements of village traders helped to defray the expenses.

86. An entry from parish magazine no. 48 of December 1870 showing how the girls of Godstone school contributed to funds.

87. Advertisement for Godstone School Printing Press, taken from parish magazine no. 43 of July 1870.

88. An advertisement in Godstone parish magazine which regularly appeared over a number of years. The following notice appeared in the March 1883 parish magazine: 'The past month has been rendered sad, memorable by an event most unexpected and most grievous. Mr. F. G. C. Edgar whose name has appeared for many years on the title page of this Magazine and who has been so well known in the place as a diligent worker in all Church and parochial matters, has proved to be a large defaulter in the parish accounts and, for very shame, has disappeared from the neighbourhood'.

89. Between the Village and Church Town, the Pest House, formerly the isolation hospital, stands at the lower end of Bullbeggars Lane.

Lords of the Manor

0. Eustace of Boulogne, one of the earliest lords to old Godstone, brought to him by his wife Goda, is epicted on the tapestry of Bayeux. His name, of which ome letters are missing (E————TIUS), appears on he top border; he points to William of Normandy, who s seated on a black charger, raising his visor to show is troops that he is alive and well. The rumour had pread that he had been killed.

91. Sir Robert Clayton (1629-1707). He turned a farmhouse into the stately mansion of Marden, here depicted in the top right-hand corner of the picture.

92. Sir William Clayton, 5th baronet, the soldier. He is depicted here as lieutenant-colonel of the 1st regiment of Bucks. Yeoman cavalry. He fought at Waterloo and became a general in 1865.

93. Marden Park before 1879, when it was burnt down. One of the Clayton ladies is on the lawn with her magnificent great dane and basket of flowers.

94. The original stables at Marden Park, which escaped the fire.

95. Marden Park, as rebuilt by the Claytons for their tenant Sir Walpole Greenwell.

96. Sir Walpole Lloyd Greenwell, 1st Bt. (1847-1919), who bought Marden Park in 1906.

97. Sir Bernard Eyre Greenwell, 2nd Bt. (1874-1939), son of Sir Walpole Greenwell.

98. Funeral of Sir Bernard Greenwell in 1939. His coffin was placed on one of the Marden drays, pulled by the magnificent shire horses bred on the estate.

99. Forestry work on the Marden Park estate in the 1940s.

100. Sowing time at Marden, *c.*1945.

101. Castle Hill, *c.*1905, on which stands an 18th-century summer house used as a hunting lodge by the Claytons. The hunting lodge has since disappeared.

102. Lagham Manor, seen here in 1908, was situated in the southern part of the parish. It was the seat of the Lucys, the St Johns, the Loveynes, the Harcourts and the Evelyns, and was occasionally held jointly with Walkhamsted, alias Godstone.

103.   Rook's Nest, which was given by the Priory of Tandridge in 1534 to Thomas Bance to hold on a 20-year lease. It passed through various ownerships after this and is seen here as it was at the time of Sir Henry Strachey (1736-1810).

104.   Rook's Nest at a later date. It was sold in 1817 to Charles Hampden Turner whose family owned it until 1928, although it was often let. Sir George Gilbert Scott lived there when he was restoring Godstone church. In 1928 J. V. Rank renamed it Oubrough, and in his time the magnificent orangery was pulled down. In 1953 he sold it to Guy's Hospital, while Strete Court School moved there two years later. The school has owned the house since 1964.

Mills

105.   A pre-1909 view of Ivy Mill, which was identified in Domesday as the mill at 'Chevington'. Godstone was an established corn milling centre using water power before the windmill era. Sluice gates in the foreground, the mill and outbuildings further along the pond can be seen. To the left is Ivy House, built by Thomas Northey the younger in 1698.

106.   Skating on Ivy Mill pond in 1908.

107. View from the western side of Ivy Mill pond, 1910.

108. Disaster struck the mill in 1909 when a heavy storm caused the bank of the millpond to burst and drain the pond. The embankment was repaired and the mill continued working until 13 October 1920 when a fire broke out, so damaging that grinding thereafter proved impossible. The pond remained until 1957, when it was drained and filled in.

109. Leigh Mill in 1895, showing the great wheel. The mill occupies an ancient site but unlike Ivy Mill is not mentioned in Domesday. It became ruinous at the time of the Black Death and was rebuilt in 1423 by Stephen and Christene att Lee who occupied a large house near the mill. In the 17th century the Evelyns used it for their manufacture of gunpowder.

110. Leigh Mill House in 1908.

111. Hilly Fields windmill is just visible in the right foreground of a water-colour preserved by a family in Redhill and now in the possession of a Bletchingley resident. The picture is a panoramic view of the country around North Park Farm seen from the south. The windmill stood on an ancient Saxon barrow behind the *Hare and Hounds*, close to Godstone Green, and was pulled down in 1876.

Transport

112. A picture taken *c*.1895.
Gentlemen of means, notably
Vanderbilt, the American
millionaire, could often be seen
on the roads from London to the
coast, driving a four in hand.

113. A double decker open-topped bus at Godstone Green, *c*.1919. It was only in 1912 that these buses superseded the horse omnibus.

114. A Green Line bus passing through Godstone Green in a picture taken in the 1920s. Between the wars and for some years after the Second World War, these buses ran every half hour between East Grinstead and Hemel Hempstead, passing through London via Victoria and Marble Arch.

115.   The station, South Godstone, showing the station buildings which have now been pulled down. This line runs between Redhill and Tonbridge. Godstone would seem to have been in an ideal situation for a line northwards to London and southwards to East Grinstead, Lewes and Eastbourne, but this was never built.

116.   A steam engine pulling into Godstone station on 15 June 1957. It is 80150 BN on the 10.18 a.m. from Redhill to Tonbridge.

GODSTONE
FIRE ENGINE ASSOCIATION.

At a Public Meeting held at the White Hart, Godstone, on Saturday, February 6th, 1841,

C. H. TURNER, ESQ. in the Chair,

IT WAS RESOLVED,

That it is expedient to establish a FIRE ENGINE for the use of Godstone and its neighbourhood.

That an Association, to be called the "GODSTONE FIRE ENGINE ASSOCIATION," be now formed for the purpose of carrying the same into effect.

That the following Gentlemen be appointed a Committee, in whom shall vest the property of the Association, and with whom shall rest the entire management of its affairs; and that three of the Committee be a quorum;

C. H. TURNER, ESQ.   MR. THOS. ROSE,
C. McNIVEN, ESQ.   MR. ED. STENNING,
LT. COL. M. LEAKE,   MR. WM. STEDALL.
JOHN PEARSON, ESQ.

That Mr. Thomas Rose be requested to act as Treasurer and Secretary of the Association.

That Mr. Wm. Stenning be requested to act as Controller of the Engine.

That subscriptions be received in aid of the funds of the Association, by Mr. Thomas Rose.

SUBSCRIPTIONS ALREADY RECEIVED.

	£.	s.	d.		£.	s.	d.
SIR W. W. PEPYS, BART.	15	0	0	C. H. TURNER, JUN. ESQ.	5	0	0
CHARLES H. TURNER, ESQ.	15	0	0	T. KENSITT, ESQ,	5	0	0
C. L. H. MASTER, ESQ,	15	0	0	REV. E. D. WICKHAM,	5	0	0
CAPT. R. WELBANK,	10	0	0	MR. THOMAS ROSE,	1	0	0
C. McNIVEN, ESQ.	10	0	0	MR. W. STENNING,	1	0	0
CAPT. FANSHAWE,	10	0	0	MR. ED. STENNING,	1	0	0
THE HON. G. H. NEVILLE,	10	0	0	MR. ALEXANDER ROSE,	1	0	0
VEN. ARCHDEACON HOARE,	10	0	0	MR. HENRY ROSE,	1	0	0
REV. W. M. PYNE,	10	0	0	MR. ED. PETERS,	1	0	0
JOHN PEARSON, ESQ.	10	0	0	MR. JOHN PETERS,	1	0	0
C. NEWBERRY, ESQ.	10	0	0	MR. W. STEDALL,	1	0	0
SIR W. R. CLAYTON, BART.	5	0	0	MR. JOHN MAWER,	1	0	0
LT. COL. M. LEAKE,	5	0	0				

[W. ALLINGHAM, PRINTER, REIGATE.]

117. Godstone Fire Engine Association was founded in 1841. In March 1850 the Fire Service became the responsibility of the Vestry and from time to time a rate was raised for its expenses. It passed to the care of civic authorities with the founding of the parish councils in 1894.

118. The early horse-drawn fire engine of the 1890s. In June 1923 the Fire Brigade were called out to a haystack fire at Bone Mill. The horses were harnessed but one flatly refused to move and lay down in the road. By 1925 a motor van was provided to tow the fire engine, but it was not until 1935 that a new motorised engine was purchased.

119. Godstone Fire Brigade, c.1919. Left to right, standing: ?, 'Buckets' Carey, John Batts, Fred Botley; seated: George Fairall, David Christie, ?.

120. The Godstone Fire Brigade in their motorised vehicle standing in front of the Leigh smithy in Tyler's Green. In the background, wearing his apron, is Charles 'Shaddy' Leigh, the blacksmith.

121. Captain George Fairall and Fred Botley, *c.*1910.

122. Fire at the *Bell*, 191●

123. Godstone St John's Ambulance Brigade, founded 1934. Founder members, standing: W. Hayward, F. H. Dumbrill, J. Cooper, J. Bailey, F. Jupp, J. Coleman; seated: W. Blackman, D. Sadler, R. Simmonds (Superintendent), C. Way, G. Campbell, A. Gocher.

24. Church Army Holiday Home, Hillbrow House, in 1909. It was situated at the southern end of the village near the *ell*. Later it became a restaurant, but has been replaced by two rows of neo-Georgian houses. The Church Army was *unded* to look after motherless children and orphans of Service and ex-Servicemen.

125.   The Ancient Order of Foresters, founded in 1867. The rector was the Hon. Chaplain. On their anniversary days, they met at the Court House for business, then formed a procession and marched to the parish church, accompanied by the band of the 7th Surrey Rifles Volunteers. They heard a sermon and then returned to dinner near the Court House.

Youth and Leisure

26. The back view of 82 High Street, where the Godstone Literary Institute, according to village tradition, first had two rooms available for its activities: this one, in an extension on the first floor, since put to other use, and a ground floor room for reading books from the parochial library, which the Vestry had made publicly available in 1855.

27. The modern Godstone Literary Institute, now the Club. The 1872 parish magazine reads: 'We commend this useful village institution to the increased patronage of those who wish to provide our rustic population with instruction and harmless amusement'. By 1873 a former brewery on Godstone Green had been converted to premises for the Institute 'on condition that they were not used as a dancing saloon or for dramatic entertainments'.

128. Horace Fairall, scoutmaster. Keenly interested in youth activities and a popular leader, he took his scouts camping in France. He also taught them much about their heritage and the history of Godstone. With his troop he compiled book, *Glorious Godstone*, published in 1934.

129. The Endeavour, the scouts' headquarters on the Green, under construction. It was Horace Fairall who inspired the work, done by the families and friends of the scouts and the scouts themselves. The framework came from the timbers of an ancient barn and the building was in Tudor style.

130.   The Endeavour was finished just before the Second World War. To the left is Pondtail, now the doctors' surgery, once the Police Station.

131.   The scouts giving an entertainment in the Endeavour: the Gang Show.

132. The Godstone Band, *c.*1906, pictured in front of the room in the *Hare and Hounds* on the Green where they used to practise. Left to right, top row: Fred Butcher, Harry Rummings, Ted Hayward, George Stevens, Bert

reatfield; middle row: Dick Ball, Bill Mayne, Bill Stevens, Arthur Stevens, Jack Killick; front row: Jack
rey, Jack Butcher, Jack Bashford, Jesse Stevens, Neddy Stevens.

133. Surrey Crest, pictured here in the 1930s, was an establishment which may be described as a holiday camp. Situated on the North Downs, it was ideal for ramblers and weekenders, and was owned by a Mr. Nunn, who had built the place between the wars. The camp survived the war though the only house in the vicinity was bombed, no trace being left. The site of the holiday home was in the path of the M25 so the bulldozers ended its existence.

Special Occasions

134. The wedding on 8 April 1912 of Rosa May Taylor of The Enterdent, Godstone, and Frederick James Hills, a baker of Epsom. The bride and bridegroom's fathers were both quarrymen.
Left to right, back row: Len Nash, Fred Gale; second row: Alma Taylor, Mary Hills, Edwin Hills, Alan Taylor, Edith Hills, W. Bates, Lilian Taylor, Rosa May Taylor, Freddie Hills; front row: ?, May Fairall, Horace Fairall, May Hills.

135. A picnic on Tilburstow Hill in 1911.

136. The Godstone Band at Godstone Place in 1912.

137. In November each year, near Guy Fawkes day, the Bonfire Boys would get up an entertainment, something like a lord mayor's show on a small scale. It was a procession representative of the various village industries. In 1909 the Maid of the Mill tableau was awarded first prize and a silver cup.

138. The village fair on the Green in Edwardian days.

139. The Sherwood Foresters marching past the *White Hart* in 1915, and along Bullbeggars Lane to St Nicholas' parish church for church parade.

Sport

140. In 1902 the need was felt for a cricket pavilion. A tramcar was purchased for £8 and a thatched roof was put on it – the whole conversion being made for a total of £35. It stood on the north side of the Green by the Bletchingley road.

141. The Godstone cricket team who played the Surrey Club and Ground team on 10 May 1913. For well over 200 years cricket has been a part of village life and the Green has been the setting for the game.

142. Godstone Cricket Club vs. Milk Marketing Board, 1947-8.

143. Godstone Football Team, 1898-9, Surrey Mirror Cup.

144. Godstone Football Club, *c.*1910. Football was started in the 1890s by the Laurence brothers, who lived at Stratton.

145. Godstone Bowls Club in the '20s. The club was founded in 1921, and started with 16 members.

Industry

146. Old mine on the east side of the old Caterham-Godstone road. This is the 'Roman Road' entrance, now blocked, which gave access to the extensive network of underground quarries below the modern A22 and to land as far east as the large warehouse in Quarry Road.

7. Hearthstone mine, near ...arden Castle, 1½ miles south-...st of Caterham station. It may ... the Winders Hill/Marden ...arry and mine, which ...pears to have been opened by ... 1850s and worked first as a ...arry for squared stone for ...ilding, and later as a mine for ...arthstone, for whitening ...ne floors, hearths and ...orsteps. During the war it ...s a security store for wine and ...rits.

148. Building-stone quarry in Upper Greensand under Godstone Hill. This can be identified as a quarry by the carefully picked smooth side walls of the quarry gallery. Another sign that this is a stone quarry rather than a hearthstone mine is the quantity of quarry waste walled up behind the dry stone wall at the far end of the gallery.

149. Hearthstone mine near Marden Park. The rough nature of the side walls on the right indicates that this is a hearthstone mine, rather than a building stone quarry. Rough blocks of hearthstone have been hacked out using hammers and wedges. There is also less quarry waste left in the galleries than there would be in a quarry.

150. The kind of pick used in Godstone quarries was known as a maddock. This sketch, taken from the notebook of G. F. Harris, a visiting geologist of 1893, shows its simple construction. Some of these maddocks were extremely heavy and were kept very sharp.

Godstone district.

Tools used.

1. The "Maddock":—

iron

steel point

sharp pick point — very sharp.

Breadth of tool across this part is called the "pod" of the maddock.

wooden wedge

(Side view)

51.   Interior of tunnel workings in the white sand of the Folkestone beds at the northern end of the village. The standing figure gives some idea of scale.

152. Entrance to hearthstone mines south of Marden Park. This photograph was taken on the occasion of a visit of the Geologists' Association on 16 June 1900.

153.   The village sandpit, *c.*1900, showing early working with carts and horses.

154. Fairall's sand diggers in the 1930s. George Fairall started exploiting the Taylor's Hill sandpit on land leased from the Turners of Rook's Nest at the turn of the century. His son, Horace, took over the business in the '30s. In the front row on the extreme left stand first Frank Hall and next to him Horace Fairall. When Horace died in 1956 Frank Hall took over as co-director with Tom Bird and Bill Carman.

155. In 1988, while preparations were being made to erect a new warehouse at Fairall's Ltd., Builders' Merchants, in the High Street, a cavern was revealed. When explored, it was discovered to measure approximately 42 by 24 ft., with spurs leading off in all directions.

Going South

156. W. G. Neal, Empire Stores, South Godstone, *c*.1905.

157. A. Hollands, Post Office and Bootmaker, South Godstone, *c*.1905.

158. South Godstone Post Office. Left to right: Mr. E. Gibbs, Mr. E. King, Mr. Sid Hollands.

159. Jack Treasure at the corner of Lagham Road and the main Eastbourne road.

160. Lagham Road, South Godstone, *c.*1906. This was known as 'New Road' in Edwardian days.

161. Station Road, South Godstone in 1905.

162.   Posterngate Farm, South Godstone, before 1912.

163.   Osney Lodge, South Godstone. A number of such gentlemen's residences were built in the countryside around South Godstone.

164. Pupils at South Godstone school in 1912.

165. The *Blue Anchor*, Blindley Heath.

166.   Gibbs' Stores, Blindley Heath.

167.   Felbridge School, *c*.1907. Founded in 1783 by James Evelyn for the instruction of poor children. Free education was given to 12 children – eight boys and four girls. They had to live within two and a half miles of the schoolhouse, which today still forms the central part of the school building and is the oldest school building in Surrey still being used for teaching.

68. James Evelyn (1718-93). A miniature by Henry Edridge from a painting by George Romney.

69. The signature and seal of James Evelyn on a deed concerning his Charity School.

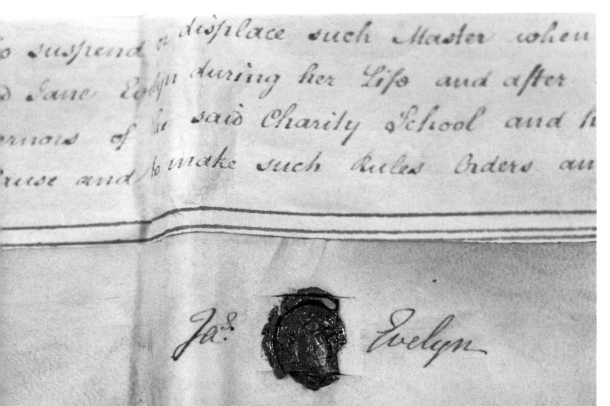

170. Children at Felbridge school in 1904 sitting on a newly-felled chestnut tree which had stood in the playground.

171. The longest-serving teachers at Felbridge scho
were Mr. and Mrs. E. F. Shaw, in charge from 1885 t
the First World War.

172. The *Star Inn*, Felbridge, 191